A New True Book

DOGS

By Elsa Posell

*This "true book" was prepared
under the direction of
Illa Podendorf,
formerly with the Laboratory School,
University of Chicago*

CHILDRENS PRESS ™

CHICAGO

196451

AKC/Dr. Barbara Howitz

Greyhound

PHOTO CREDITS

American Kennel Club (AKC)—2, 14 (left), 15 (left), 16 (right), 20 (lower left), 21, 23, 24, 29 (left), 32 (2 photos), 34, 37, 40, 44

Art Thoma—7, 9 (left), 20 (top), 29 (right)

Candee and Associates—9 (right), 13, 15 (right), 19 (left), 27 (2 photos)

Lynn M. Stone—Cover, 10, 14 (right)

Julie O'Neil—12, 16 (right), 20 (lower right), 26, 31

Carson and Barnes Circus—19 (right)

Tony Freeman—42

James P. Rowan—4, 39   Cover-Golden Retriever

Library of Congress Cataloging in Publication Data

Posell, Elsa Z.
  Dogs.
  (A New true book)
  Previously published as: The true book of dogs. 1961.
  Summary: Briefly discusses a variety of hunting, sporting, working, non-sporting, and toy dogs and how to choose and care for a dog as a pet.
  1. Dogs—Juvenile. [1. Dogs] I. Title.
SF426.5.P67   1981   636.7   81-7742
ISBN 0-516-01614-8   AACR2

10 11 12 13 14 15 16 17 18 19 20 R 99 98 97 96 95 94 93 92

TABLE OF CONTENTS

DOGS, DOGS, MORE DOGS

There are many kinds of dogs. There are large dogs, small dogs, tall dogs, and short dogs. There are dogs with long hair and dogs with short hair. All of them are loved by the people who own them.

DIFFERENT KINDS OF DOGS

People who know about dogs have divided them into six groups.

Two groups of dogs are good hunting dogs.

Another group—the terriers—were once hunting dogs but now they are kept for pets.

There is a group of dogs that work.

The last two groups of dogs are neither hunting dogs nor working dogs. They stay close to their masters as pets or to protect them.

All these different dogs can be good pets.

DOGS ARE SMART

Have you heard someone say "A dog is man's best friend"? Most dog owners feel that this is true. Dogs try hard to please their owners.

A dog is easy to train. It can learn many things. It can learn to work and to help people.

Weimaraner

Irish setter

A dog knows people, places, and things by their smells and sounds. A dog can often find its way home if it is lost.

A dog can hear a sound long before people can hear it. A dog can hear sounds people can't hear. It even knows from which direction it came.

Pointer

HUNTING
OR SPORTING DOGS

BIRD DOGS

Bird dogs are one kind of hunting dog. They help hunters find birds. They get the scent of birds from the air.

A pointer is a hunting dog. It gets its name from the way it stands and shows a hunter where there is a bird on the ground.

Labrador retriever

Retrievers are good swimmers. They bring back birds that have fallen into water.

Bird dogs help hunters. They look for quail, pheasant, wild ducks, or geese.

Retrievers help hunters look for birds.

English cocker spaniel

Golden retriever

There are many hunting dogs. These dogs sometimes are called sporting dogs.

HOUNDS

Hounds are hunting dogs, too. Hounds follow the scent on the ground. They help hunters find deer, foxes, rabbits, and other animals.

There are many different kinds of hounds.

Left: Beagles
Right: Afghan hounds

AKC/Joyce Hart

Left: Scottish terrier
Right: Irish terriers

TERRIERS

Years ago terriers were used to hunt foxes, gophers, badgers, and other small animals. Terriers are no longer hunters. They are, more often, pets.

Most terriers are not
large. They learn tricks
quickly. They are brave
and often pick fights with
bigger dogs. They are very
playful. Sometimes their
play is rough.

There are many kinds of
terriers. When trained well,
a terrier makes a good
city pet. City dogs need
less food and exercise
than some other dogs.

WORKING DOGS

Eskimo dogs have thick coats to keep them warm. Their wide feet are padded. This helps the dogs travel over snow and ice. At night they curl up in the snow, put their noses under their tails and sleep without being cold.

An Eskimo dog is a good hunter. It will fight a polar bear if it must.

Alaskan malamute,
an Eskimo dog

Paulette's Peerless Puppies,
performing circus dogs

Some dogs perform on
the stage or in a circus.
These dogs learn to dance,
to climb ladders, to jump
through hoops, and to do
many other tricks. It takes
a long time to train a dog
for show business.

Collie

Great Dane

Old English sheepdogs

AKC/John Ashbey

Most working dogs are large animals. They are strong and able to learn many things.

Belgian and English sheepdogs, the German shepherd, and the Scotland collie are good workers.

Working dogs take care of cattle and sheep on ranches.

Working dogs will chase away wild animals. They will find an animal that is lost. Working dogs help the rancher drive animals where he wants them to go.

In Belgium and Holland, dogs once pulled carts. They brought milk or vegetables to market.

Great
Dane

Great Danes and boxers are good watchdogs.

The Doberman pinscher and the German shepherd are sometimes trained to help the police.

Newfoundland

Newfoundland dogs are good swimmers. They often save people from drowning.

A German shepherd makes a good Seeing Eye dog. Its training begins when it is 15 to 18 months old. It takes 3 to 5 months to train a Seeing Eye dog.

The Seeing Eye dog learns to obey a blind master. But it will not obey if it will get the master into trouble. A master trusts the eyes of his dog.

Once dogs worked with soldiers. Because of their fine sense of smell, dogs were able to find men who were hurt. They saved many lives.

Dogs carried war messages. They kept rats and other pests away from the soldiers, too.

German shepherds have gone into battle with many soldiers.

St. Bernard dogs were once sent out, two at a time, to help people lost in the snow in the mountains. When the dogs found a person who needed help, one dog stayed with him and kept him warm with its body. The other dog would go for help.

NON-SPORTING DOGS

Dogs that are not used for hunting or working are called non-sporting dogs.

The chow chow is a non-sporting dog. It is the only dog with a blue and black tongue. A chow is seldom friendly with anyone but its master. It is a good watchdog, but it is not always a good pet for a family.

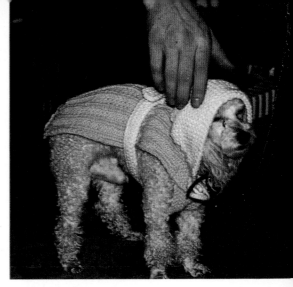

Left: Chow chow puppy
Right: Poodle

AKC/Jayne Langdon

A poodle makes a good pet for people who live in small houses or apartments. A poodle is easy to train and needs little exercise. Its thick coat grows fast and must be clipped and brushed.

A bulldog may look fierce, but it is a gentle, friendly animal. It seems to know when it is loved. A bulldog is patient even though some thoughtless children may tease it.

There are many non-sporting dogs.

Yorkshire terrier

TOY DOGS

Some dogs are so small that they are called toy dogs.

The Chihuahua often weighs as little as one pound.

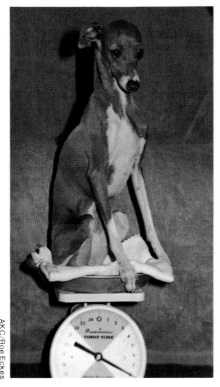

Left: Italian greyhound
Right: Maltese

A Pomeranian often weighs less than five pounds. It will probably never weigh more than eight pounds.

Even toy dogs often make fine watchdogs.

TAKE CARE
OF YOUR DOG

A dog of your own is a
wonderful pet. Be sure that
you are willing to take
care of it.

You must feed a dog
and give it fresh water and
a clean place to sleep.
You must brush, exercise,
and train your dog.

A dog is worth all the time you give it. A dog will be your loyal friend if you are good to it.

Choose a dog that will suit you and your family.

If you live in the country where a dog can run, you might choose one of the bigger kinds of dogs.

A small, short-haired dog makes the best pet if you live in a city. It eats less, sheds less hair, and needs less exercise.

If you get a puppy, you can train it the way you want it trained. A puppy should be eight or ten weeks old before it is taken from its mother.

Smooth fox terrier

Before you bring your dog home, fix a place for it to sleep. A box with an old pillow or a piece of an old blanket in it will make a good bed. Be sure your dog understands that this bed is where it must sleep.

Have two dishes ready for your dog—one for food and one for water.

Puppies less than four months old are fed four times a day. When they are from four to six months old, they are fed three times a day. When a dog is about a year old, it is fed twice a day. Most dogs are fed only once a day by the time they are two years old.

Your dog does not need a bath often. A daily brushing with the right kind of brush is best for it.

Your dog must have shots to keep it well. Take it to the veterinarian. The vet will tell you a lot about dog care.

Golden retriever puppies

You can begin to housebreak your puppy as soon as you bring it home.

Feed your puppy at the same time every day. Take it out as soon as it has eaten. If you can't take the puppy out, fill a box with torn newspapers for it to use.

Never run after your dog to catch it. The dog will think that you are playing and run off. Hold out your hand and call or whistle softly. When your dog comes to you, pat it and give it a dog biscuit or a bit of food that it likes. Do this over and over.

You can teach your dog to obey many simple commands in this way. You can teach your dog to sit, to stand, to come, and to do other tricks for you. A well-trained dog is a joy to everyone.

Poodle

Most dogs whose parents and grandparents were good dogs are raised in kennels. They may cost a lot of money.

Many dogs that are not thought to be such good dogs make wonderful pets. They do not cost as much, even at a pet store. Some people get a dog from the city pound or from a friend whose dog has puppies.

AKC/Terry Bednarczyk

The dogs you have been reading about are different from each other. They are all alike in certain ways, too. They all have fur, four legs, sharp teeth, and good ears, eyes, and noses. They all can be trained to be good pets.

WORDS YOU SHOULD KNOW

badger (BAJ•er)—an animal that lives underground and has short legs and thick fur

Belgian sheepdog (BEL•jin sheep dog)—a type of dog that was raised in Belgium and used to herd sheep

Belgium (BEL•jum)—a country in Europe

boxer (BOCKS•er)—a dog with a short, square face and a short, smooth brown coat

brave (BRAIV)—having courage

bulldog—a dog with a large head, thick body, short legs, and short hair

Chihuahua (chih•WAH•wah)—a very small dog

coat (KOHT)—fur or hair of an animal

chow chow—a medium-size dog with a thick coat and a blue-black tongue

collie (KOLL•ee)—a large dog with long hair and a narrow face

command (kuh•MAND)—give orders to

different (DIF•ih•rent)—not the same; unlike

divide (dih•VYD)—separate

Doberman pinscher (DOH•ber•man PIN•sher)—a large dog with a smooth brown or black coat

drown—to die under water because you don't have air

Eskimo dog (ES•kih•moh dog)—a strong, medium-size dog with a thick coat which is used for pulling sleds

fierce (FEERSS)—dangerous

German shepherd—a large dog with a black or brown coat

gopher (GO•fer)—a small animal that lives in burrows in the ground

Great Dane (GRAIT DAIN)—a large dog with a short, smooth coat

group—a number of animals, persons, or things that are together

Holland (HOLL•end)—a country in Europe

hound —a dog with drooping ears and a good sense of smell that is used in hunting

kennel (KEN•il) —a place where dogs are kept

loyal (LOY•il) —faithful; stand by

master —a person who owns an animal

Newfoundland (NYU•fund•lend) —a large, strong dog

obey (oh•BAY) —to do what you are told

pad —a small, soft part on the bottom of the feet of some animals

patient (PAY•shunt) —to wait quietly; not to complain

perform (per•FORM) —to do something that others enjoy watching

pheasant (FEZ•unt) —a large bird with bright colors and a long tail

pointer (POYNT•er)-a dog with a short, smooth coat that is used in hunting

polar bear (POH•ler behr) —a large white bear that lives in the far north

Pomeranian (pom•er•AY•nee•un) —a small dog with long hair, ears that stand up, and a tail which is carried over the back

poodle (POO•dil) —a dog with thick curly hair

pound —a place where stray dogs are kept

quail (KWAYL) —a small bird with a short tail

rancher —a person who raises cattle, sheep, or horses

retriever (ree•TREE•vir) —a dog that is trained to find and bring back animals which have been shot

scent (SENT) —a smell; odor

seldom (SEL•dum) —not often

St. Bernard (saynt ber•NARD) —a very large dog that was used to help travelers in the mountains

terrier (TAIR•ee•yer) —a dog that is small and active

thoughtless (THAWT•less) —without thinking

train (TRAYN) —to teach

trust —depend on

veterinarian (vet•rih•NAIR•ee•un) —an animal doctor

INDEX

About the author

Elsa Posell received her M.S. in Library Science from Western Reserve University. She has been a librarian in the Cleveland Heights Public Schools, and is currently devoting over half her time to work with children in the Cleveland area and other Ohio counties in language arts, story telling, and creative writing. As a story teller and lecturer Mrs. Posell has worked in schools in Korea, Japan, Hong Kong and China. One of her books, This is an Orchestra, *is published in Japanese. Mrs. Posell is also the author of* American Composers, Russian Music and Musicians, Russian Authors, *and* Beginning Book of Knowledge of Seashells.